FIGHTING INVISIBLE TIGERS

A Stress Management Guide For Teens

FIGHTING INVISIBLE TIGERS

A Stress Management Guide For Teens

Earl Hipp

Edited by Pamela Espeland
Illustrated by Troy Acker

Free Spirit
PUBLISHING

Library of Congress Cataloging-in-Publication Data

Hipp, Earl, 1944-
   Fighting invisible tigers.

   Bibliography: p.
   Includes index.
   Summary: Discusses the pressures and problems
encountered by gifted students and provides information
on life skills, stress management, and methods of
gaining more control over their lives.
   1. Youth--United States--Life skills guides--Juvenile
literature. [1. Stress (Psychology) 2. Stress
(Physiology) 3. Gifted children. 4. Life skills]
I. Title.
HQ796.H495   1985   305.2'35   85-80632
ISBN 0-915793-04-0 (pbk.)

10 9 8 7 6 5 4

Printed in the United States of America

Cover and book design by Nancy MacLean and
Michael Tuminelly

Free Spirit Publishing Co.
123 North Third Street
Minneapolis, MN 55401

The perfectionism scale pages 107-108 has been reprinted
with the permission of *Psychology Today Magazine*.

DEDICATION

To H.P. for making it all possible.

ACKNOWLEDGMENTS

Thanks to my publisher, Judy Galbraith, for her continual support and her willingness to share her commitment to the young people she serves. The hope that the system will someday change to allow for the full development of human potential is kept alive in people like her.

Thanks to my editor, Pamela Espeland, for her patience, sense of humor, and wizardly skills.

Thanks to the kids who took a risk to share of themselves so intimately and freely.

Thanks to all those who remained available and supportive throughout the writing of this book.

And thanks to Picole for her presence and patience as I work on my dream.

CONTENTS

INTRODUCTION

Have any of these words come out of your mouth lately? Check the statements that sound as if you might have said (or thought) them.

☐ I feel underchallenged in school. I'm bored!
☐ Sometimes life is TOO MUCH TO TAKE (what with getting up at 5:30 a.m. to study for tests, competing in gymnastics, taking piano lessons, feeling lonely, fighting with my parents and sister, babysitting my little brothers, getting depressed, and/or _____).
☐ It's hard to feel okay about myself when people make fun of me just because I'm smart/different/me.
☐ I can't seem to make and keep friends. There must be something wrong with me.
☐ I'm afraid of failing.
☐ Too many people expect too much from me.
☐ My teachers are set in their ways and dull, dull, dull.
☐ I have trouble keeping up with everything I'm supposed to do.
☐ I'm just not happy with myself or what I'm doing. In fact, I'm just not happy, period.

If you checked some (or most, or all) of these, you're not alone. Other talented, bright, and competent teenagers have told us that they're bothered by the same things.

We surveyed hundreds of teens, and what we learned was that most of them feel overwhelmed, frustrated, frightened, and in some cases victimized by the many challenges in their lives. They feel STRESSED OUT.

It's getting harder and harder to be a kid. Few get by without paying some physical or emotional price for living with stress. And the more talented you are, the more you pay. Heightened sensitivity, creativity, and intellectual potential can make it particularly difficult to live in our changing, challenging, demanding world.

Here is what other kids said when we asked them to describe how they felt under stress:

"Emotionally confused, mentally exhausted, physically hyper."

"Tired, drained, fat, ugly, pushed by others, back pains, can't sleep, listless, depressed."

"I get headaches. I feel like I am in a tightly closed box."

"I feel like blowing up and tearing the room apart."

"Shaky, wanting to withdraw, helpless, like crying."

"Frustrated and worn out, sick, angry, like screaming."

"Down, mad, stupid, alone, nothing."

"Grouchy, moody, bored with life."

"I feel like I am going to break."

Being under stress is like being inside a ball of rubber bands. The pressure in there is *tremendous*. And whenever you add another rubber band (a stressor), the pressure increases.

Human beings have limits to the amount of internal pressure they can stand. When you're living close to your limit, life can feel scary, overwhelming, depressing, and downright dangerous.

It can feel like a jungle where tigers stalk you day and night.

Ferocious tigers. Hungry tigers. Invisible tigers.

Imagine that you're alone in a steamy, spooky jungle. You've been hacking through it for days while huge mosquitoes chomp at your flesh. Weird noises and strange smells fill the air, and you've felt enough heat to fry your brain. And every now and then you've heard a deep, menacing growl.

Now imagine what it would be like to live with this anxiety every day. You'd have to be constantly watchful, on edge, and ready to react.

How could you possibly use your full potential? How could you be your best self? How could you avoid feeling cranky and tired all the time?

And what if you had to stay in the jungle for years and years?

When this much stress goes on for that long, it can lead to depression, illness, and even death. Chronic stress is serious business.

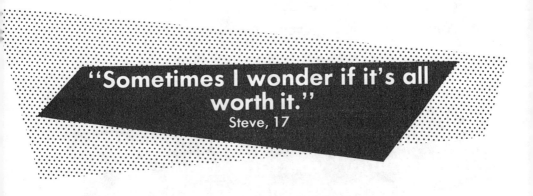

"Sometimes I wonder if it's all worth it."
Steve, 17

THE BAD NEWS

◆ You can't cure stress by thinking or worrying about it.

◆ Being bright, talented, creative, motivated, smart, ambitious, and even good looking can add to the stress in your life.

◆ Academic success and drive aren't enough to make life manageable. The world is too complicated and intense, and it's changing too fast.

◆ There are no easy answers, simple solutions, or quick fixes for managing stress.

◆ Only a handful of families and schools teach the lifeskills you need to successfully deal with stress.

So, what can you do to keep from being wounded or gobbled up in your journey through the jungle?

THE GOOD NEWS

● You *can* learn to understand why your life gets oppressive, depressive, stressed or otherwise unhealthy.

● You *can* learn to live in a new and better way.

● You *can* feel more in charge of your world.

● Even a small change in your lifestyle can make a big difference.

> "If the only tool you have is a hammer, you tend to see every problem as a nail."
> Abraham Maslow

ABOUT THIS BOOK

Fighting Invisible Tigers is more than just a survival guide to life under demanding conditions. It's a mini-course in becoming the best person you can be. Hundreds of young people just like you helped to write it.

Part I, "Life in the Jungle," will help you to . . . .

. . . understand your physical and emotional responses to stress,

. . . see some common misconceptions kids have that *guarantee* trouble,

. . . identify healthy and unhealthy ways of dealing with stress, and

. . . recognize the difference between coping and stress management.

Part II, "Lifeskills," will teach you to . . . .

. . . exercise more control over your life,

. . . formulate a measure of "success" that's right for you,

. . . be more confident and have more self-esteem,

. . . make and keep good friends,

. . . express anger and other feelings in positive ways,

. . . develop a program for getting physically healthy,

. . . understand the value of play, humor, and having fun, and

. . . strike a balance between the things that make for successful living.

The goal is to give you some tools you can use to create a better life for yourself.

The hope is that the resources described in this book, combined with your potential for growth and hunger for new experiences, will result in a better you — someone who's well-equipped for the adventure of life and likely to experience more of the joy and satisfaction that life can offer.

Good luck and have fun!

Earl Hipp

FIGHTING INVISIBLE TIGERS

You may think that stress is a modern phenomenon, but that's only because there's been so much talk about it lately. Actually, it was around as long ago as four million B.C., when our ancestor Australopithecus (handsome devil, and could he dance!) was struggling to survive.

Our cave dwelling forebears had a tough life: fires that wouldn't start, spoiled meat, trouble with the neighbors, and no television. But worst of all were the animals that regarded them as food. On any given day, a huge sabertooth with lunch on its mind could sneak up on our poor relative.

THE FIGHT-OR-FLIGHT RESPONSE

That drooling tiger was in no mood for conversation, so A. Pithecus had to learn to react *right away* and either bash the cat or flee for his life. This required a finely-tuned nervous system that could instantly mobilize the body into what we now call the "fight-or-flight" response. Prehistoric people who *didn't* have it became tasty snacks for predators. Those who *did* lived on. (Today's tigers are still referring to them as "the ones that got away.")

The process of natural selection has gifted you with a marvelous, miraculous nervous system. It can get your body moving, and moving *fast*, at the first hint of danger. It's so sensitive that just thinking about tigers can be enough to get your whole system fired up.

While you may never have to face a real tiger, the world you live in can feel every bit as perilous as the one of millennia ago. It can be downright scary to . . . .

· · · get a poor grade on a test,
· · · watch your parents have a blow-out fight,
· · · see a friend get drunk or high on drugs,
· · · think about Life After High School (in the Real World),
· · · and/or consider the possibility of nuclear war.

Whenever you're up against something that makes you feel threatened, it's just like meeting a hungry tiger. Off goes the alarm, and your body prepares to slug it out or run!

It helps to understand the changes that take place inside you during anxious moments. Together they comprise a sort of "early warning system," a set of signals indicating that corrective action should be taken.

It also helps to know that it's *perfectly normal* to feel strange physical sensations in times of stress. Your body isn't malfunctioning; instead, it's working just as it should.

Here is a picture of some of the changes that take place in healthy bodies during the fight-or-flight response. (Different people will experience them to a greater or lesser degree.)

What's amazing about these changes is that they're *instantaneous* and *completely automatic*.

WHAT HAPPENS	WHY IT HAPPENS
Your heart pounds.	*The body needs all of the oxygen-rich blood it can get, and it needs it in a hurry, so the heart beats harder and faster.*
Your hands and feet feel cooler than usual.	*The capillaries in them constrict to make more blood available at the center of the body and in the large muscles needed for running and fighting.*
You may feel warm in the face, your cheeks and ears may get pink, and/or you may suddenly develop a "pressure" headache.	*The carotid arteries in the neck open up to allow more blood to the brain.*
Your mouth may get dry and/or you may have an upset stomach.	*The digestive tract shuts down to let its blood be used elsewhere.*
You may get "butterflies" in your stomach and/or feel "high."	*Glands and organs produce chemicals that help the body to prepare for running or fighting. The most common of these is adrenaline.*
You sweat. Your hands may get clammy.	*Anticipating the extra heat that running and fighting generate, the body turns on its climate-control system by producing excess moisture on the surface of the skin. Evaporation of this moisture creates a cooling effect.*

> **"Virtually every organ and every chemical constituent of the human body is involved in the general stress reaction."**
> Dr. Hans Selye in *The Stress of Life*

COMING DOWN

The fight-or-flight response takes a lot out of you. Luckily it doesn't last forever. It's usually followed by a "coming down" period, and then a return to normalcy.

Here is a picture of the *short-term stress pattern:*

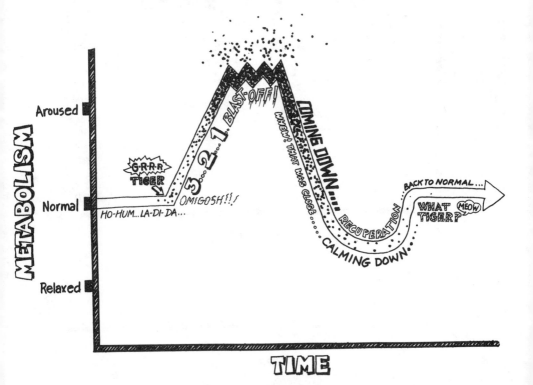

SHORT-TERM STRESS

CRASHING AND BURNING

What happens when we live with stress all the time and never come down far enough to fully recover? We learn to adapt to gradually increase pressures until we're living with an *unhealthy* amount of stress and calling it normal. The longer we do this, the closer we come to crashing and burning.

Here's a picture of the *long-term stress pattern*:

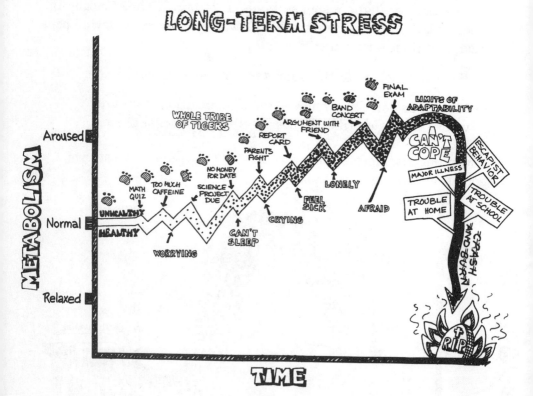

Some of the reasons behind long-term stress include:

◆ We experience so many stressful events in our lives that it isn't practical (or possible) to recuperate after each one.

◆ We are the products of a "driven" culture. We're taught that it's *good* to hurry, win, compete, and always be productive.

"The trouble with the rat race is that even if you win, you're still a rat."
Lily Tomlin

◆ Most of us don't know how to relax. Relaxation skills aren't valued by our culture, so hardly anybody teaches them.

Even our attempts at play are filled with pressure to perform. Recreation becomes wreckreation!

Later on, we'll talk about how to develop relaxation skills. For now, just be aware that the world you live in expects (and prefers) you to be up and moving rather than down and relaxing. We're told that going faster and working harder is the key to feeling better.

The trouble is, *it isn't*. So we end up feeling that life is hopeless, full of worry, and no fun.

Smart kids are especially good at adapting to demanding circumstances. The more conscientious and responsible you are, the harder you'll try to do a *great* job of handling everything.

Here are some things that other kids do in an effort to keep things together:

"I try hard to learn one more thing."

"I skip meals."

"I cut out my play time."

"I NEVER tell anyone how I feel. They might think I'm not smart after all!"

"I go it alone."

"I make time for one more project."

Obsessed with the need to appear bright, competent, and "together," performance-oriented people don't notice when it's becoming more and more difficult to get things done.

It's like the woodcutter who never stops to sharpen his axe — and has to work harder to do what used to be easy.

HOW TO TELL WHEN YOU'RE REACHING YOUR LIMIT

As you keep piling on the stressors, you may not be aware that your ability to meet the demands of life is eroding. You'll continue to plug away, make room, make time, adapt — and you'll start heading straight toward physical and emotional problems.

You'll also experience a variety of symptoms indicating that you're nearing your limit. Here are some that other kids have reported:

- More trouble with teachers

- Needing a lot of sleep, or not being able to sleep

- Feeling hungry all the time (and putting on weight), or never eating

- Headaches, stomach aches, colds, infections, sore muscles

- Overdoing it on one type of activity (too much T.V., music, study)

- Withdrawing from friends and family ("Just leave me alone!")

- Crying for no apparent reason

- Feeling like a jerk

- Restlessness, anxiety, worrying

- Feeling like the world is out of control

- Depression, grumpiness, the blahs

These symptoms may seem to come out of the blue. You'll be busy adapting and trying to cope — and all of a sudden you'll find yourself doubling over with stomach cramps . . . or tossing and turning at night . . . or yelling at your mom . . . or biting your nails . . . or downing whole crates of corn chips . . . .

WARNING! WARNING! APPROACHING SYSTEM OVERLOAD! SHUT DOWN NOW TO AVOID SERIOUS DAMAGE

IF LIFE IS SUPPOSED TO BE
SO MUCH FUN,
WHY DO I FEEL SO SAD?

TROPICAL ILLUSIONS

There is no stress in the world. REPEAT: There is no stress in the world.

Surprised? Think about it. Where would you go looking if you wanted to find some stress? The Gobi Desert? South Wales? Chengtu, China?

Stress is something that happens inside you. It's a product of how you perceive, define, and react to the world.

You're not convinced? Try putting yourself into these two scenarios:

1

You're at the circus, having a great time, when all at once the ringmaster announces that YOU have been chosen to fill in for the lion tamer (who's out with the flu). You think it's a joke until several strongmen climb up the bleachers toward you, hoist you up onto their shoulders, cart you down to the lion's cage, open the door, and toss you inside. You look at the lions, the lions look at you (licking their chops), and your body screams "FIGHT OR FLIGHT!"

2

Same thing: you're at the circus minding your own business, and suddenly you get the news that you're Lion Tamer for the Day. But hey, no big deal! You've been to lion-tamer school. So you have the skills and experience you need to do the job.

In each instance, the lions are the same. The difference lies in whether you perceive them as dangerous or manageable.

What you see is what you get. If you see the world as full of lions (or tigers) out to tear you to pieces, you'll spend every day under stress and on edge. Your body will perpetually be in a fight-or-flight state — which leads to physical and emotional exhaustion.

FEARS AND MISCONCEPTIONS

How do *you* perceive the world? What are *your* fears, rational and irrational? Think about this for a moment, and then list them here.

I am afraid . . . .

_____   _____

_____   _____

_____   _____

_____   _____

_____   _____

Bright, creative kids like yourself tend to have overactive imaginations. Their fears are complex, colorful, and detailed.

It would be great if bright, creative kids like yourself were also better equipped to handle their fears and problems, but that's not always the case. Instead, they often make things harder on themselves by setting up barriers — misconceptions that stand in the way of success.

12 MISCONCEPTIONS THAT GUARANTEE TROUBLE

1. I can think my way out of feeling bad.

2. I must be crazy for thinking/feeling the way I do.

3. If I just keep busy, I'll eventually feel better about myself.

4. If I tell (my mom, my dad, my school counselor, a friend) about how I feel, he/she won't care or understand.

5. I have to do EVERYTHING by myself — including dealing with my fears and problems. I can't ask anyone for help.

6. It is NOT okay to cry.

7. If I can just get through today, tomorrow is bound to be better.

8. Because I'm smart, I should be able to figure things out by myself.

9. Life is so serious!

10. All I need is to be left alone for a while.

11. I don't have time to eat right, relax, or play.

12. Other people always know what's best for me.

Do any of these sound familiar to you? Can you tell what's wrong with each of them?

Misconceptions slow you down — and give your tigers a chance to gain on you.

WORRY TAPES

Worries are another way to make things worse for yourself. Like endless-loop tapes, they play your fears and misconceptions over and over in your mind. They create the *illusion* that you're working on your problems. But all they really do is take up your time, tense up your body, drain your energy, and ruin your attitude. *They don't improve your life one bit.*

Yet many smart and talented kids have a headful of worry tapes — about grades, about fitting in, about the future, about their bodies, about having friends.

"I have to get an A in advanced calculus, no matter what. But I'm not sure I can . . . . What if I don't?"

"My parents are fighting again. They've been fighting a lot lately. Maybe this means that they're going to get a divorce . . . . What if they do?"

"I want to go to the dance. But I'm afraid that I'll do something stupid, like trip over my feet and fall on my face . . . . What if I do?"

These tapes drown out the sounds of their own good sense and the voices of people who are ready, willing, and able to help.

The next time you catch yourself in the middle of a worry tape, try turning it off. The switch is just inside your right ear.

Seriously: There *is* a way to deal with feeling bad or anxious. It's called *coping*. It's not bona fide stress management, but it can afford a temporary measure of relief.

DEALING WITH THE FEELING: HOW KIDS COPE WITH STRESS

Stress is unavoidable. To survive, we must come up with ways to lessen the pressure from *too much* stress long before it reaches the bursting point.

When we asked kids how they cope with stress, here is what they said:

"I read a new book or write in my diary." (Mary, 14)

"I stomp around the house and pound on my brother." (Tim, 15)

"I ignore it until it blows over." (Sharon, 16)

"I punch a pillow and cry." (Jennifer, 12)

"I get away from it all with my friends." (Holly, 17)

"I listen to the white noise of blank tapes until I've calmed myself down." (Lynn, 16)

"I talk to myself." (Dan, 14)

"I stay organized and on top of things." (Melissa, 16)

"I watch TV and eat, eat, eat." (Nan, 15)

"I play the piano, go for a walk, or take a bath." (Tina, 15)

Coping is a *short-term* approach to dealing with the *feeling* of being stressed. In other words, it can't heal what ails you. All it can do is mask your discomfort and help you to *stop* feeling for a while — to "get by" for a little longer. There's nothing wrong with that, as long as it doesn't go on forever.

But it's easy to string coping activities together and put off feeling crummy for hours or even days. Then it becomes a lot like using your finger to plug up a leak in a dam. It works for a moment — and then the growing pressure behind the dam breaks through in another leak, and then another. At some point, you run out of fingers!

There are three main types of coping strategies: *distraction*, *avoidance*, and *escape*. Some of the activities within these strategies are healthy, and some are not. It all depends on *why* you use them and *how long* you use them.

DISTRACTION

Watching TV, phoning a friend, eating, listening to music, taking a bath, going for a walk, reading a book, even studying can all be distractions. Each is a way to temporarily put off facing the anxieties of life.

There's no problem so big that you can't run away from it -- at least for awhile.

Distractions are the shortest-lived and least drastic of coping activities. Most of them are also pretty harmless.

AVOIDANCE

Avoidance activities are distractions carried to an extreme. They take up more of your time and energy and enable you to sidestep your troubles for longer periods.

Joining the chess club can be a healthy distraction, but joining the chess club *and* the debating society *and* the drama club *and* the school orchestra may add up to avoidance. Listening to music can be a distraction, but going everywhere with your headphones on is probably an avoidance.

Avoidance activities may look good from the outside. For example, we know a student who *seems* very successful. He's very busy with classes and clubs. He's in advanced math, advanced physics, a special class for high-achievers, and an honors group,

in addition to being on his school's Quiz Bowl team. It's hard to find fault with someone like that!

What people *don't* see is how lonely he is. He'd like to make friends, but he doesn't have time. He'd like to relax and have fun, but he doesn't know how. The only way he can keep his grades up is by studying constantly.

He's living in a VICIOUS CIRCLE. The more he studies, the lonelier he gets. The lonelier he gets, the more he studies to mask his feelings of loneliness. The more courses and clubs he gets involved in, the more he worries about keeping up, and the less time he takes for enjoying himself and making friends.

A vicious circle closes in on you from all sides, growing tighter and tighter — like a noose.

There are four other avoidance activities that have the potential to become vicious circles: *procrastination, illness, sleep,* and *withdrawal.*

"Avoidance is only a vacuum that something else must fill."
Shirley Hazzard in *The Bay of Noon*

Procrastination

Everyone procrastinates. Some of the smartest, most motivated, and most successful people in the world today are known (or secret) procrastinators.

When it comes to dealing with stress, however, procrastination can be dangerous. It's like slowly shaking a can of soda. It continues to look the same from the outside, but pop the tab and POW!

Occasional procrastination is simply a bad habit. Regular procrastination is a problem. Leaving too many projects on the back burner can work against your competency and eventually paralyze you.

"Procrastination is the art of keeping up with yesterday."
Don Marquis in *archy and mehitabel*

Illness

Interestingly, parents are usually the ones who teach kids how to use illness as a way out. When they let us stay home from school in the early days, we learned how nice it could be. Being waited on by mom, drinking 7-Up to settle our stomachs, and watching as much TV as we wanted were powerful reinforcers.

Now that you're older, it's still tempting to revert back to those times. It's easy to go from feeling pressured to feeling queasy, and to wanting someone else to "fix things" for you — like your mom.

Watch it! Like procrastination, getting sick can become a habit. Unlike procrastination, it can have serious consequences for your body. The longer you're sick, the lower your resistance becomes, and the more vulnerable you are to attacks from itinerant germs.

In our culture, being ill is an honorable excuse for just about anything. Nobody expects you to solve your problems when you're flat on your back. But they won't go away just because you refuse to face them, and prolonged stress can actually *reduce* your ability to combat germs.

Sleep

Hating to get up on Monday mornings and going down for an occasional nap are both perfectly normal. The difference between sleep as an ordinary function and sleep as an avoidance activity is all a matter of degree. Even people who do hard physical labor don't need 10 hours a night every night.

The more you sleep, the more your problems pile up, the more anxious you become, and the more you want to sleep. When your eyelids start drooping at the sight of a couch, you're running away from something!

"Preserve me from unreasonable and immoderate sleep."
Samuel Johnson in *Prayers and Meditations*

Some kids claim that as their troubles get worse, they become more susceptible to gravity. Who's winning in your life — you or it?

Withdrawal

As stressors gather and growl, it's natural to want to get away. In fact, withdrawing from the world to regroup and recoup can be a positive move.

It's when you close your door and *never come out* that it's time to start worrying. When withdrawal leads to isolation, when you're alone a lot and angry or scared, your self-confidence begins to erode. If you don't feel good about yourself, your competency dwindles — and you're smack in the middle of another vicious circle.

ESCAPE

If avoidance is distraction taken to an extreme, escape is avoidance gone amok. Escapist behaviors signal that you've reached the limits of your ability to cope.

Here is how other kids describe it:

"I just want to leave and get away from everything and everyone." (Lynn, 16)

"I feel like my head is being squeezed into a 1" x 1" cube." (Karen, 16)

"It's like being on the brink of laughing or crying hysterically." (Kelly, 15)

"It makes me weak." (Al, 10)

Severe escapist behaviors include:

● skipping school or dropping out,
● running away from home,
● caving in to the system (accepting mediocrity or less),
● abusing alcohol or other drugs,
● becoming a video games junkie, and/or
● developing a food addiction.

Escapism is the point at which coping becomes crazy. Escapist behaviors generate whole mountains of additional problems that can burden a person for life.

If you're leaning toward any of these, GET HELP. Find someone you can talk to — a parent, a friend, a school counselor. And don't feel embarrassed about it. Asking for help BEFORE you're in trouble is a sign of a psychologically healthy person.

Coping with stress is short-term fix — like putting a band-aid on a wound. If all you have is a tiny scratch, a band-aid should do it. But if you're walking around with tiger bites, band-aids aren't the answer.

What you need are *stress management* skills. They're different from coping strategies because they actually *reduce* the overall amount of pressure in your life and help you to deal with challenges in healthy ways.

Imagine that you're back in front of that leaky dam. Now imagine that you can lower the water level behind it and simultaneously make the dam stronger.

That's what stress management is all about. Now let's find out how to do it.

TAMING YOUR TIGERS

Coping is great in emergencies, but it's no way to live. If you're tired of feeling tiger-breath on the back of your neck, stress management offers a better way. It enables you to eventually tame your tigers and make the jungle your playground.

Successful stress management requires something called *life-skills*. Lifeskills are tools that can help you do more than just deal with the feeling of being stressed. They can actually give you more control over your attitude, your self-esteem, and the quality and direction of your life.

There's nothing difficult or mysterious about them. Anyone can learn them. Anyone can use them. All it takes is practice.

Here's what you'll need to get started and keep going:

▶ **A supportive environment.**
Talk to your parents and teachers. Let them know that you're planning to make some changes in your life. (Your parents or siblings may want to join you!)

▶ **A structured learning program.**
Set aside some time for practicing and perfecting these lifeskills. Make up a schedule — and follow it.

▶ **Lots of patience.**
You'll notice a difference in your life almost immediately, but don't expect large-scale miracles overnight. If you've spent the past few years fighting invisible tigers, not all of your stress will disappear in an instant.

▶ **A ton of self-acceptance.**
There's nothing wrong with the way you are — but imagine how good it will feel to become even *more* competent and capable!

"No limits but the sky."
Miguel Cervantes in *Don Quixote*

TAKING CARE OF #1

Since stress is something that happens inside you, it's logical to begin your stress-management program by learning to take better care of your body and your mind. Exercise, diet, and relaxation are all important to your well-being.

There are several "self-care" skills that can reduce stress and make living more enjoyable. They're easy to acquire, they offer a fairly quick return, and you can do them on your own.

USE IT OR LOSE IT

In most schools today, physical education is limited to five hours a week of aggressive, competitive, jocks-and-socks, win-or-lose activities. Few make the team, and the rest get to watch and take showers.

We make heroes out of athletes and shame everyone else with required and largely irrelevant classes that are ordeals for those who aren't the athletic type. It can feel awful to participate in something that doesn't make sense to you. Plus — even worse — you get graded!

"I got a B in phy-ed even though I did everything everybody else did. I even took showers. When I asked the teacher about it, he said, 'You've already got all A's, and I'm not going to give you another one.' Talk about unfair!"
Rick (14)

In order to reach your full potential, your body *must* be physically active on a regular basis. Getting (and keeping) your body in shape has a direct effect on your energy level, health and longevity, appearance, self-esteem, and self-image.

But since the schools probably aren't going to do much for you in this area, you're going to have to do it yourself. And this involves two straightforward steps:

1. Find a form of physical activity that you enjoy.

2. Participate in a way that facilitates a long-term, self-loving, nonabusive commitment.

In other words, figure out what you like and then stick with it.

Notice that we haven't mentioned the word "exercise." For most people, exercise means sweat, work, discomfort, and even pain. ("Feel the burn!" "No pain, no gain!")

"I meet many people who get all fired up to begin an exercise program, only to give up after a few weeks. Inevitably, the reason turns out to be that they selected an exercise not suited for them or that they over-exercised, or both."
Covert Bailey in *Fit or Fat?*

Almost *any* kind of *steady* physical activity will do. If you like to walk, walk. If you love to swim, swim. If you have to run, run. ANYTHING is better than sitting and thinking about it. You do enough flexing of your brain cells. Now get your body moving!

FIT is an acronym that can make you a whiz at putting one foot in front of the other in a way that feels right for you. The "F" stands for *frequency*, the "I" stands for *intensity*, and the "T" stands for *time*.

Frequency

The *minimum* required to *maintain* your fitness level is three sessions of physical activity per week. Improving it will take more.

By three sessions, we don't mean three hours in a row on Mondays and nothing for the next six days. Instead, spread your physical activity out over the week.

Regular activity lets your body know that you're serious about getting in shape. Time off in between sessions gives it a chance to rest and rebuild.

Intensity

Our culture worships results over process. As you embark on your program, you'll be tempted to go faster and be better than everyone else. If you can't find someone to compete with, you'll compete with yourself and push yourself to improve. And you may burn out before you've had the opportunity to burn up some of that excess fat.

To keep your good intentions from going down the drain, start by finding your own appropriate intensity level. There are two ways to measure this: by determining your *target heart rate*, and by whistling while you work.

Your target heart rate is the *specific* pulse rate that offers you the *maximum* benefit during periods of physical activity. (Contrary to popular belief, working harder isn't better.) You can figure yours out with this formula:

$$\frac{(220 - \text{your age}) \times 70\%}{6} = \text{your target heart rate}$$

(NOTE: The top part of the formula determines your target heart rate per minute. You divide it by six because in checking your pulse you only count for 10 seconds. After that, a healthy heart begins to return to its normal rate.)

Now determine how close you come to your magic number. Spend about 20 minutes on your chosen physical activity, and then check your pulse at your wrist or at the carotid artery alongside your Adam's apple.

 If you're ABOVE your target heart rate, you're pushing yourself too hard.

 If you're BELOW your target heart rate, you're taking it too easy.

 If you're AT (or very close to) your target heart rate, you've achieved your appropriate intensity level.

Whistling while you work — the second measure of appropriateness — is preferable if you're just beginning to be physically active. It's also very simple. Basically, if you can whistle (or sing, or carry on a conversation) while you're being active, you won't be at risk of overdoing it.

Is overdoing it a problem? Probably not in terms of *physical* danger, since you're young. But it isn't fun and it doesn't feel good. If you keep it up, you may eventually give it up, and you'll be right back where you started.

Time

To get the most out of your physical activity, you need to keep your heart rate in its target zone for 20-30 minutes, *nonstop*. A getting-it-up-there, letting-it-drop cycle won't do it.

That's why swimming, walking, jogging, and jumping rope are better fitness sports than tennis and softball. You need to start moving and keep moving, uninterrupted, for about half an hour. Use the time before and after for warming up and cooling down.

To sum it all up, FIT = 3 sessions each week of a physical activity you enjoy, with 20-30 minutes of target heart rate each session.

What are the benefits of the FIT approach? Here are just a few:

■ As your metabolic functions improve, your body uses the calories it consumes more efficiently. It gets better at burning fat.

■ Because your body gets better at burning fat, you get (or stay) slim and trim.

■ Your attitude improves. You feel more mellow, more relaxed.

■ Your heart, lungs, muscles, and other vital parts get stronger and better at what they do. As a result, you may add 2-10 years to your life.

■ Remember the chemicals your body produces during the fight-or-flight response? Being physically active is a form of "taking flight" and using them up in a positive and healthy way. It actually helps to *relieve* stress.

Not bad for such a small investment of time and effort!

If you want to know more about "getting physical" (and find out interesting facts like why bathroom scales don't tell you anything about fat), read:

Fit or Fat? by Covert Bailey (Boston: Houghton Mifflin Co., 1978)

The New Aerobics by Kenneth H. Cooper (New York: Bantam Books, 1981)

Planning for Wellness by D. Ardell and M. Tager (Oregon: Wellness Media, Ltd., 1981)

YOU ARE WHAT YOU EAT

For many teens, the four basic food groups are Fast, Sweet, Carbonated, and "everything else," and it's the last category that includes the sensible, nutritious stuff. The average kid's diet is long on the first three.

If you've had biology, you may recall that every cell in your body is affected by what you eat — skin cells, muscle cells, blood cells, nerve cells, brain cells. If you don't treat them right, they'll get their revenge in one way or another.

While healthy eating is a major lifeskill that takes time, commitment, and study, there are two big problem areas that you can address right now: your caffeine consumption, and your sugar consumption. Regular use (or overuse) of these substances can make you *feel* crazy even if the rest of your life is in perfect order.

Hippity-Hop

When we asked kids, "Do you use caffeine?", here is what some of them said:

"Pot after pot after pot." (Daniel, 17)

"Not much — a couple of colas, maybe 4 or 5 cups of coffee a day." (Tanya, 16)

"I take four caffeine pills every morning to get through the day." (Rochelle, 15)

Most of the students we surveyed reported some use of caffeine — and many reported a lot. That's bad.

Caffeine in its pure state is a white, bitter-tasting, crystalline substance that belongs to the group of naturally occurring stimulants called *methylxanthines*. Methylxanthines are found in coffee beans, tea leaves, kola nuts, cocoa beans, and a few other plants.

Why is caffeine a problem? Because it elicits a physical reaction very similar to the fight-or-flight response. Too much of it makes you edgy and jittery. It also turns up the volume on your worry tapes so things seem worse than they are.

Caffeine is "hidden" in all sorts of things — chocolate, cold capsules, cough syrups, even yummy hot cocoa. But the biggest villain as far as kids are concerned is probably soda pop. Unless the can says "caffeine free," be prepared to pay the price!

Some of the signs of excess caffeine intake include restlessness, nervousness, irritability, the shakes, sleeplessness (or scary dreams), an irregular heartbeat, increased frequency of urination, stomach upsets, intestinal disturbances, and an irresistible desire to hippity-hop all over the place.

If these sound like the symptoms of excess stress, that's because they're very similar. When you're hyped up on caffeine, it's hard to tell whether your anxieties are due to your upcoming English exam, the fight you just had with your dad, or the drug you've been consuming — because caffeine *is* a drug.

The students we surveyed reported another caffeine-related hitch: headaches. Tension headaches (head pains caused by either vascular pressure or muscle tension) can result from too much stress — or too little caffeine, if your body is used to regular doses. Like many other drugs, caffeine is addictive, and its sudden absence can trigger withdrawal symptoms.

Depending on your body size and chemistry, it's possible to get hooked on caffeine at consumption levels between 200-400 milligrams per day. That's equivalent to four cans of regular cola or four cups of coffee.

How can you tell if you're a caffeine fiend? Try going without it for a few days. If you get a headache, and if a cup of coffee or a can of cola relieves it, you've got trouble.

You may be amazed to learn that America's favorite headache pain relievers are loaded with caffeine. They give temporary relief — while quietly increasing the intensity of your addiction. Strange but true.

Riding the Sugarcoaster

Sugar by any other name — glucose, sucrose, fructose, or corn syrup — tastes as sweet. And no matter what form it takes, it can generate subtle (and sometimes not-so-subtle) mood swings. It can leave you feeling giggly one moment and in need of a nap the next.

Because processed sugars are so chemically simple, your body absorbs them into the bloodstream very quickly. This gives you a wonderful buzz that can brighten the end of a gloomy and boring day (hence the 3:00 candy bar craving) and light up your life . . . for about an hour.

What's behind the "sugar high"? The sudden boost in blood sugar surprises your pancreas. The average pancreas is relatively imperturbable, but it tends to overreact when the sugar alarm goes off. It starts secreting insulin, which traps the excess sugar in the blood and carries it to the liver. The liver then goes into high gear and starts removing the excess sugar.

But it doesn't know quite when to stop, so it removes *too much* blood sugar — which sends you back down toward the doldrums. You get sleepy and cranky, so you make another trip to the vending machine.

You've just strapped yourself into the front seat of the sugar-coaster. Up (sugar rush), down (sugar crash), up (sugar rush), down (sugar crash) — and on and on it goes. Each crash takes you deeper than the last.

A single can of regular cola is equivalent to half a sandwich bag full of white sugar. BIG up, BIG down. But the cola folks are no dummies, so they add caffeine to help prolong the rush.

One chemical picks you up and later drops you off a cliff into mild depression. Meanwhile, the other strings you out with artificial energy that gives you headaches and exaggerates your problems. Some fun!

Question:

How much sugar does the average American consume each year?

Circle one:

15 pounds   37 pounds   63 pounds   128 pounds

(The answer is printed upside-down on the bottom of the page.)

"Sugar is like puppy love that makes your teeth rot."
Scott Knickelbine in *The Low-Cost No-Fuss All-Natural Food Guide for Students (And Other Desperate People)*

Our culture supports the idea that it's okay to use chemicals to feel better. It's hard *not* to use caffeine and sugar when they're so readily available and made to appear so innocent. *But it's not impossible.*

If you can't go cold turkey on either (or both) of these substances, at least reduce your intake.

● If you simply MUST stay up late to study, try some brief periods of stimulating physical activity to get your blood

128 pounds

52

flowing to your brain. Run in place or do jumping-jacks. If you can't get along without the taste of coffee, drink decaf.

 If your sweet-tooth starts throbbing, munch on fruit. (An apple is NOT a ticket to the sugarcoaster because the sugars it contains are of the complex natural variety that your body breaks down slowly.)

Rabbit Food and Self-Esteem

Can lettuce make you a better person? Can carrots give you courage? You may find it hard to believe, but . . . yes. Not only because of what they can do for your body, but also because of what they can do for your mind.

It's all tied in with habits. Every one of us is at the mercy of the collection of habits called "my life." This ragtag assortment has as much momentum as the giant cruise ship Queen Mary. Once it gets going, it takes a long time to slow it down or change course.

The captain knows that and doesn't try to turn it on a dime. But we often forget that it takes just as long to change the way we live. We try to make it happen too fast — and we run into the powerful force of habit, which usually knocks us flat.

If you've ever tried to lose weight, start an activity program, or quit biting your fingernails, you know how hard it can be. Giving up breeds a sense of failure that wreaks havoc on your self-esteem.

So — back to rabbit food. Eating lettuce and carrots (and spinach and parsley) is good for you. It's a *positive* activity. If you do it regularly, you can say, "I do positive things for myself and am growing in positive ways." It's almost *too* simple.

The trick to overcoming the force of habit is to make minuscule changes and stick with them. Eating a salad instead of dessert for one day a week can allow you to identify yourself as someone who's growing in a positive way. Snacking on carrots instead of candy for one day a week can improve your self-esteem and make you a mysterious and fascinating person. (Maybe that's an exaggeration. Then again, maybe not. Try it and see!)

"... it is a peaceful thing to be one succeeding."
Gertrude Stein

DON'T YOU THINK YOU'RE OVERDOING IT ON THE CARROTS, RALPH?

Being physically active and eating right have definite benefits for your body. But what do they have to do with stress?

Plenty. Once you start working off your nervous energy and stop consuming jet fuel, the world will appear to slow down and feel less intimidating. Some problems won't loom as large, and others may disappear altogether.

Life is always throwing curveballs, however. So the lifeskills that make you healthy aren't all you need to succeed. For those times when the world around you seems to be falling apart, you'll want a reservoir of relaxation skills. Those come next.

If you want to learn more about eating right, read:
The Low-Cost No-Fuss All-Natural Food Guide for Students (And Other Desperate People) by Scott Knickelbine (Manitowoc, WI: Natural Press, 1983)

FINDING THE EYE OF THE HURRICANE

We all have moments when life feels overwhelming. It's as if we're caught in a hurricane somewhere out on the ocean, rocked by waves of emotion, dashed by demands from everyone around us, and blown about by the moods and opinions of others. We wonder if our fragile constitutions will weather the storm.

For times like these, we need a whole new set of skills. We need to know how to find the eye of the hurricane — that zone of relative calm at its center where the sun shines and the wind settles down to a breeze.

Relaxation skills can take us there. They can help us to achieve a deep quiet in mind and body, a nourishing psychophysiological peace.

There are many different types of relaxation techniques, but they all have these three characteristics in common:

1 They must be learned, and that means they must be practiced.

2 They result in noticeable, measurable physiological changes.

3 They involve a focus of attention on something other than "thinking."

Essentially, relaxation is *nondoing* — something a lot of people find difficult. The goal of every relaxation strategy is to be physically still while maintaining an alert but neutral mental state. Other words that describe the experience include *allowing*, *passive attention*, and *focused rest*.

Knowing how to relax is essential to maximizing your potential and maintaining your brain in tip-top shape. Refusing to relax is like keeping the muscles in your arms constantly tensed. Eventually you'll lose flexibility, feel fatigued, and find it hard to do simple, everyday things like writing, brushing your teeth, and waving goodbye.

Without periods of relaxation, you lose your abilities to think straight and concentrate — much less generate brilliant or creative ideas.

Here are some things kids said they did to relax. See if you can sort out the real relaxation techniques from the coping strategies (short-term dealing with the feeling) and the activities that are no help at all. Identify each using these letters: "C" for coping, "R" for relaxation, and "N" for no help. (The answers are printed upside-down on the bottom of the page.)

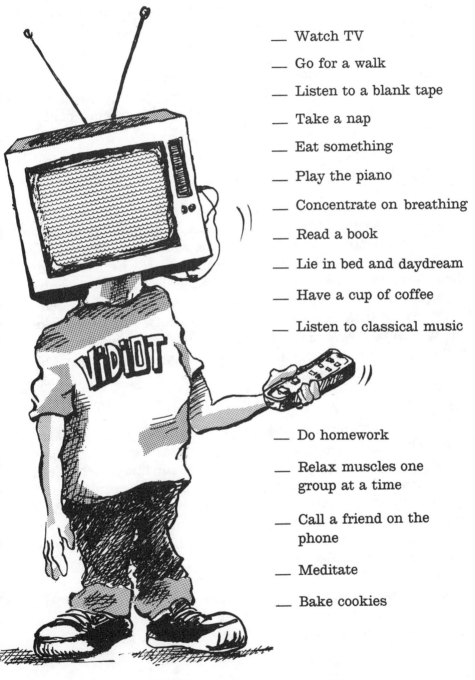

___ Watch TV

___ Go for a walk

___ Listen to a blank tape

___ Take a nap

___ Eat something

___ Play the piano

___ Concentrate on breathing

___ Read a book

___ Lie in bed and daydream

___ Have a cup of coffee

___ Listen to classical music

___ Do homework

___ Relax muscles one group at a time

___ Call a friend on the phone

___ Meditate

___ Bake cookies

Did you discover that some things you thought were relaxation techniques were actually coping strategies — or no good at all?

■ Watching TV is *not* a relaxation technique because your brain is busy, your mental focus isn't neutral, and the TV is in charge.

■ Sleep is *not* a relaxation technique because it isn't a controlled state and you're not alert during it. Plus dreams (especially nightmares) can cause physical and emotional stress.

■ Reading a book is *not* a relaxation technique because your mental focus is on the printed page.

Remember that coping strategies can make you feel better by temporarily masking anxiety and tension. In contrast, relaxation takes you directly to the calm eye of the storm.

What were the real relaxation techniques in the list above? There were only three: meditating, listening to a blank tape, and concentrating on breathing. All are forms of *nondoing*.

There's no trick to learning relaxation skills. But it *does* take practice. In fact, your ability to relax will be directly proportionate to the time you devote to practicing very simple nonactivities. Following are two for you to try.

Deep Breathing

Your body and mind function together. (An ulcer is a good example of what can happen when things upstairs go wrong.) Your thoughts and feelings affect your physical condition; conversely, your physical state can influence your attitude and mood.

When you're nervous, excited, or angry, your breathing is more rapid than usual and tends to move up in your chest. When you're calm and relaxed, your breathing is slow and regular and located further down. Slow, deep breathing is the physical equivalent of a peaceful mind.

It's possible to *consciously* manipulate your breathing to achieve a restful mental state — even during times of stress. The script that follows will show you how. (You may find it helpful to have someone you trust read it to you until you feel ready to go it alone.)

You'll need something comfortable to lie on — a thick rug, or an exercise mat.

PREPARATION:

 Lie on your back and let your toes point outward so your legs and hips relax.

 Loosen any restrictive belts or clothing.

DEEP BREATHING SCRIPT

Keeping your mouth closed, inhale and exhale deeply through your nose three times. Now place your right hand on your stomach, just above your belly-button, and your left hand on your chest. Don't try to manipulate your breathing yet, but do notice where in your trunk your breath is located.

Now take a long, slow, deep breath into your chest. Your left hand should rise, but your right should stay still. Pause briefly, keeping your chest full, and then exhale slowly through your nose.

Notice which muscles are involved, the sensation of fullness at the pause, and the feeling of relaxation that comes with the slow, deliberate release of air.

Repeat this three times. In . . . pause . . . out, in . . . pause . . . out, in . . . pause . . . out.

Now take a break. Stop controlling your breathing and let it find its own rhythm and place.

Now repeat the same steps, only this time breathe into your stomach. Your right hand should rise while your left remains still. This "belly breathing" will feel awkward at first, but be patient.

59

Ready? In . . . pause . . . out, in . . . pause . . . out, in . . . pause . . . out.

Take another break and let your breathing revert to its natural state.

Now, keeping your hands in place, combine all of these breathing movements into one slow, continuous, four-count exercise, like this:

◆ Count "one" and breathe into your belly so your right hand rises. When you're completely full, pause for a mini-second.

◆ Count "two" and breathe into your chest so your left hand rises. Pause for another mini-second.

◆ Count "three" and begin a controlled, gradual exhalation from your stomach so your right hand lowers. When the air feels half out, pause again for a mini-second.

◆ Count "four" and slowly release the remaining air in your chest so your left hand lowers. When your whole body feels empty, pause one last time.

Repeat this cycle for two to three minutes.

Finally, let your breathing return to normal.

Go through the whole script three or four times until you feel comfortable with it. From then on, use the four-count cycle as your main breathing exercise.

When you know what you're doing, lengthen your sessions. (You may want to use a timer.) With practice, the four movements will blend together and become more-or-less automatic. You will then be able to call on this skill whenever you want to enter the calm eye of the storm.

This exercise provides immediate benefits and is easy to learn. It's often taught in childbirth education classes to help women deal with the stress of giving birth. It may help you to "give birth" to tests, tough assignments, and solutions to conflicts with friends or family.

> **"Nothing can be more useful to a man than a determination not to be hurried."**
> Henry David Thoreau

Meditation

Just as your heart beats endlessly, day in and day out, your mind produces an endless stream of thoughts. If you don't believe this, try putting a stop to your thinking. Set this book down, close your eyes, and turn off your brain.

(PAUSE)

Did it work? No — because it simply can't be done. Your brain is a regular thinking machine! Even when you try to create a quiet space, thoughts keep elbowing their way in.

The only way to get some relief is by *purposefully* focusing your attention somewhere else. To relax, you must concentrate on something neutral. That's the goal of any meditation exercise.

The instructions that follow can help you to detach yourself from your thinking machine.

PREPARATION:

◎ Find a firm chair and a blank wall to look at.

◎ Sit on the chair facing the wall, with your back relaxed but straight. (This position may feel uncomfortable at first, but it's easier on your back in the long run.) Your feet should be flat on the floor.

◎ Fold your hands in your lap or lay them flat along the tops of your thighs.

◎ Keeping your head upright, tuck your chin back and in.

◎ Keep your eyes open and look down at about a 45-degree angle. (Don't tilt your head.) You should be staring at the blank surface of the wall in front of you.

This is the basic training posture. When you assume it, you become one of a company of meditators all over the world.

MEDITATION HOW-TO

All this meditation exercise involves is counting your breaths. There are only three rules to remember:

• Don't try to manipulate your breathing; just let it come naturally.

• Don't move your body.

• Don't stop before the designated time is up.

Decide *before* you start how long you want to spend meditating. In the beginning, 5-10 minutes is about right. Later you may want to lengthen your sessions; a sensible upper limit is half an hour.

When you're ready and comfortable, begin.

Keeping your mouth closed, inhale and silently count "one" . . . Now exhale and silently count "two" . . . Now inhale and silently count "three" . . . Now exhale and silently count "four" . . . and so on up to ten. On the next inhalation, start over with one and continue counting to yourself. Whenever you reach ten, go back to one again.

Nothing sounds simpler than breathing and counting, right? Actually, meditation is more difficult than it appears. The moment you begin, you're likely to encounter a whole series of roadblocks.

Roadblock #1: Your Rebellious Mind

What happens: Your mind won't take kindly to your attempts to control it. It's accustomed to being the boss and keeping busy. So it will generate subtle and distracting thoughts, and before you know it you'll have forgotten all about counting. The thinking machine will be back in charge.

Bright kids — for whom thinking is a primary survival activity — seem to have the most trouble with this. Your slick and tricky mind will try anything to get you off track: "reminders" of things you have to do, interesting and creative thoughts, sexy thoughts, bothersome thoughts.

What to do: As soon as you realize you've been distracted, go back to "one" and start counting again.

The first few times you try meditating, you may barely get beyond "one." That's okay!

"It will take quite a long time before you find your calm serene mind in your practice. Many sensations come, many thoughts or images arise, but they are just waves of your own mind . . . . [If] you are not bothered by the waves, gradually they will become calmer and calmer."
Shunryu Suzuki, Zen Master

Roadblock #2: Your Rebellious Body

What happens: Your body isn't used to being still while you're awake. In the beginning, it won't like it. So it, too, will do its best to distract you. Body parts will "demand" to move. Discomfort will threaten to become unbearable pain. A twitch will come out of nowhere; an itch will drive you crazy.

What to do: Go back to "one" and start counting again.

All of these bodily distractions are the result of a restless mind. No matter how compelling a physical sensation may seem, *it will go away* if you return to the count.

To date, no one has developed gangrene, paralysis, or any other serious physical problems because of sitting still!

Roadblock #3: The World

What happens: The whole world seems to know when you're about to start meditating — and it seems dead set on preventing you from doing it. Friends call or stop by, people knock on your door, your little brother barges into the room, or the next-door neighbor picks that particular moment to mow the lawn.

What to do: Go back to "one" and start counting again.

Unless you join a monastery, you'll *never* find absolute quiet. So you have to learn to ignore distractions.

It may help to choose a time when you can be reasonably sure of not being interrupted. (Five minutes before dinner isn't a particularly good one.) You should also choose a place that's off the beaten track — like your room, provided you don't share it with 17 siblings. You may want to make a "Do Not Disturb" sign and hang it on your door.

Meditation is one of the greatest relaxers around. It slows down many of your body processes, including your heart rate and your breathing. It empties your mind of all sorts of extraneous garbage. It settles and calms you from head to toe.

People who meditate regularly also claim that it gives them enormous amounts of energy, both physical and mental. Letting go of old thoughts and worry tapes makes room for wondrous and interesting new ideas. Try it and see!

"If your mind is empty, it is always ready for anything; it is open to everything."
Shunryu Suzuki, Zen Master

If you want to know more about developing relaxation skills, read:

Zen Mind Beginners Mind by Shunryu Suzuki (New York: Weatherhill, Inc., 1973)
How To Relax by John D. Curtis and Richard Detert (California: Mayfield Publishing, 1981)
The Relaxation & Stress Reduction Workbook by Martha Davis, Matthew McKay, and Elizabeth Robbins Eshelman (California: New Harbinger, 1980)

Four Good Reasons To Practice Relaxation Skills

You've mastered the art of relaxation. You're so good at it that you can practically turn yourself to jelly just by *thinking* about your breathing.

So what? Will the ability to relax get you good grades, expensive presents, awards, or dates with movie stars?

Not in this life it won't. But it *will* do lots of other things for you. Including (but not limited to) these:

1 Relaxation skills will help you feel less crazy, worried, and insecure. Getting control of your mind and body is a big and important step, and one that you should feel proud of.

2 Relaxation skills will give your body a chance to rest and recover from the stresses and strains of everyday existence.

3 Relaxation skills will enable you to catch up, settle down, and recenter yourself.

4 Relaxation skills will help you to feel *good*.

And when you leave the eye of the hurricane, you'll take a little calm with you on your journey through the jungle.

BEING ASSERTIVE

Do you ever feel victimized by your parents, teachers, or the world in general? If so, you're not alone.

"School is an exercise in people abuse."
Polly (18)

There are two basic reasons why young people feel oppressed:

1 Some schools and teachers, friends, and family members are flat-out bananas at times. They victimize kids intentionally and unintentionally.

2 Most kids lack the skills they need to defend themselves against crazy people and situations. (By failing to offer this kind of skills training, schools innocently *prepare* students to be victims.)

You can plan on regular encounters with people and situations that make no sense. And unless you learn to speak up and express your feelings in constructive ways, you may be trapped in Bananas Land forever!

How good are you at sticking up for yourself? Find out by taking this quiz. Answer each question with a Y (for yes) or an N (for no).

— When a teacher is unfair, do you call it to his/her/someone's attention?

— When a friend is very (or regularly) late to meet you, do you mention it?

— When you're in line for lunch or a movie and someone cuts in front of you, do you speak up?

— Do you confront kids who embarrass you?

— If someone borrows something of yours and keeps it for too long, do you ask for it back?

— When someone owes you money, do you ask for it?

— When a friend has trouble (like a death in the family), are you able to express your feelings and be supportive?

— When your teacher makes an error in class, are you able to speak up about it in a noncritical way?

— Do you feel comfortable when you're the only teen in a group of grownups?

— If you wanted to see a play and none of your friends were interested, would you go by yourself?

If you answered "no" to more than a couple of these questions, you need some assertiveness skills! More about those in a moment. But first, let's consider the alternatives.

Most kids respond to oppressive or demanding circumstances in one of three ways: by being *passive,* by being *aggressive,* or by being *passive-aggressive.* As we look at each, see if any seems familiar to you.

THE PASSIVE RESPONSE STYLE

Passive people try to function under crazy demands without making anyone mad at them. As a result, they don't get their needs met and they end up feeling inadequate, misunderstood, pressured, angry, and more than a little bit crazy themselves. They talk, behave, feel, and sometimes even look like victims.

Your economics teacher gives only four As per semester. Rather than tell her how unreasonable the system feels to you, you work like a demon to get one of those As — and feel ripped-off and anxious every time you go to class.

Your parents demand that you study for two hours every night, no matter what. Instead of trying to negotiate with them, you do what they say, grit your teeth, and stuff your anger.

A friend has borrowed a book of yours, and you need it back. He calls and asks if it's okay to keep it for another two weeks. You say "Sure, no problem," and then complain about him to your other friends.

The passive person quietly endures, puts up with, suffers through — and gripes. Over time, victims learn to be better victims. They go through life attracting things that oppress and depress them.

"An appeaser is one who feeds a crocodile — hoping it will eat him last."
Winston Churchill

69

Why are some people passive? Because . . . .

. . . they don't know how to be assertive,

. . . they fear the loss of approval and support from others,

. . . they want to avoid conflict and keep the peace at all costs,

. . . feeling like a victim is all they know, and they're afraid to change,

. . . they mistake passivity for politeness,

. . . they mistake assertiveness for aggressiveness,

. . . they are uncertain about their basic rights, and/or

. . . somewhere along the line, they've been rewarded for being passive.

Passiveness has a price, and it's a steep one in terms of stress and self-esteem. Passive people give up their sense of worth and value. They have difficulty establishing close relationships. They lose the respect of others. They don't get their needs met. They experience emotional pressure and tension. They're basically insecure, lonely, and resentful.

> "A man who trims himself to suit everybody will soon whittle himself away."
> — Charles M. Schwab

THE AGGRESSIVE RESPONSE STYLE

Aggressive people are loud, abusive, and sarcastic. They flaunt authority, argue, gossip, tease, and put people down when they feel oppressed. Because they're no fun to be around, people don't like them, which makes them even crazier.

Your English teacher gives you a C on a paper because you wrote it by hand instead of typing it. Rather than explaining that your typewriter broke, you tear up the paper in class and leave the scraps on his desk.

Your parents have set a 1:00 a.m. curfew for a night when all of your other friends are planning a beach party until dawn. You throw a fit and decide to stay home "just to show them."

Someone cuts in front of you in the lunch line. You shove her out of the way and call her a rude name.

Why are some people aggressive? Because . . . .

. . . they fear appearing weak or losing control of the situation,

. . . they need to dominate, win, or get their way all the time,

. . . they don't know how else to act,

. . . they mistake aggressiveness for assertiveness.

Like passiveness, aggressiveness costs. Aggressive people lose the respect of others and are shunned by them. They don't enjoy close relationships. They feel misunderstood, guilty, or remorseful and experience ongoing emotional and physical symptoms of stress. And they don't get their needs met, either.

THE PASSIVE-AGGRESSIVE RESPONSE STYLE

Passive-aggressive people manage to combine the worst attributes of both passiveness and aggressiveness. When they're angry, they exact their revenge in subtle and sneaky ways.

Your algebra teacher makes an error in grading your final exam. You accept it meekly — and return to the classroom after school to glue his desk drawers shut.

Your parents order you to mow the lawn on a day when you've made other plans. You smile, agree, and then go out to the garage and deliberately damage the lawnmower.

A friend arrives late for a movie. You put on a stony face and say almost nothing for the rest of the evening.

Passive-aggressive people are angry, but they don't know appropriate ways to show their anger. Instead of getting their needs met, they get revenge! They never let other people know how they feel. As a result, their friends are often frustrated with them, and resolving interpersonal problems is nearly impossible.

While no one is a purely passive, aggressive, or passive-aggressive personality, each of us has a dominant tendency. You may be aware of yours, or you may have to ask someone else what you're like.

We mentioned assertiveness earlier; now let's define it.

ASSERTIVENESS — THE ANSWER

Assertive behavior allows a person to communicate feelings honestly, directly, and openly without feeling anxious or acting like a jerk. Assertive people behave in ways that get their needs met without compromising anyone else's rights.

Being assertive is a skill that takes knowledge and practice — knowledge of your basic rights, and practice for proficiency.

YOUR BASIC RIGHTS

- You have the right to make decisions about your life
- You have the right to say "no" to the demands of others
- You have the right to respond to people who criticize you or put you down
- You have the right to share feelings about anger and fear, as well as love and joy
- You have the right to respond to violations of your rights

Here are a few more especially for students, taken from *The Gifted Kids Survival Guide (For Ages 11-18)* by Judy Galbraith:

- You have a right to attend classes which are as interesting as they are challenging
- You have a right to do your best work when you want to and less than perfect work when you don't
- You have a right to be different
- You have a right to pursue relevant schoolwork at your own speed.

Practicing Assertiveness

A formula conveniently called **"ASSERT"** can help you get started communicating your feelings, exercising your rights, and responding appropriately to violations of your rights.

- The "**A**" stands for "**Attention.**" Before you can solve your problem, you first have to get the other person to agree to listen to you.

- The first "**S**" stands for "**Soon, Simple, Short.**" Try to respond as soon as you realize that your rights have been violated. Keep your response simple, brief, and to the point.

- The second "**S**" stands for "**Specific Behavior.**" Focus on the *behavior* that compromised your rights, not the person who used the behavior.

- The "**E**" stands for "**Effect on Me.**" Share the *feelings* you experienced as a result of the behavior.

- The "**R**" stands for "**Response.**" Describe your preferred outcome and ask for some feedback.

- The "**T**" stands for "**Terms.**" If all goes well, you should be able to make an agreement with the other person about how to handle the situation in the future.

Here are three examples of **ASSERT** in action:

I. THE PROBLEM: A teacher who announces grades out loud in class.

ATTENTION: "Miss Smith, I want to talk to you about something that's a problem for me."

SOON, SIMPLE, SHORT: "It's about something that happened this afternoon."

SPECIFIC BEHAVIOR: "You announced everybody's grades in class."

EFFECT ON ME: "When you do that, I feel angry. I feel that my performance should be between you and me."

RESPONSE: "Would you be willing to use another method of distributing grades? It's really very important to me."

TERMS: "From now on, I'd like to get my grades from you before class starts. And I'd like you to agree not to make my grades public without my consent."

II. THE PROBLEM: A "friend" who always wants help with his homework. (This one happens to smart kids a lot.)

ATTENTION: "Bobby, would you be willing to sit down and talk for a few minutes about something that's been bothering me?"

SOON, SIMPLE, SHORT: "This morning, when you asked me to help you with your homework again, I realized that it made me very uncomfortable. It's something we need to talk about."

SPECIFIC BEHAVIOR: "When you ask me for help so often, I feel like you're taking advantage of our friendship."

EFFECT: "I get angry and worry that it might come between us."

RESPONSE: "I'd appreciate it if you wouldn't ask so often. Maybe you could ask the teacher to suggest someone else who could help you."

TERMS: "It's okay, then, for me to tell you when I'm reaching my limit of wanting to help? And you'll find other people to go to?"

III. THE PROBLEM: A parent who complains about a B when the rest of your report card is As.

ATTENTION: "Mom, I need to talk with you about something that's bothering me. Do you have a minute now?"

SOON, SIMPLE, SHORT: "It's about the comments you made last night about the B on my report card."

SPECIFIC BEHAVIOR: "I have a problem with you focusing on the B and not recognizing the work and effort that went into the As."

EFFECT: "It makes me feel angry, and feel like I have to be perfect in order to get your approval and support."

RESPONSE: "It would be much more encouraging for me if you would celebrate with me for doing the best I can, no matter what grade I get."

TERMS: "Next semester, will you try to support me regardless of my grades? You can ask me how I feel about how I'm doing."

The ASSERT formula isn't foolproof. It won't always work, and you won't always change the world for the better. But you will create an opportunity for the world to meet your needs by expressing them openly and effectively. By minimizing your defensiveness (and offensiveness), you'll clear the way for honest communication.

Plus you'll be able to stop "stewing in your own juice." Letting your feelings out is like an emotional "safety valve" that keeps things from reaching the bursting point.

"No one can make you feel inferior without your consent."
Eleanor Roosevelt

If you want to know more about assertiveness training, read:

Your Perfect Right by Robert E. Alberti and Michael L. Emmons (San Luis Obispo, CA: Impact Publishers, Inc., 1982)

The Assertive Woman by Stanlee Phelps and Nancy Austin (San Luis Obispo, CA: Impact Publishers, Inc., 1975)

When I Say No I Feel Guilty by Manuel J. Smith (New York: Bantam Books, 1981).

Wellness Workbook by Regina Ryan and John Travis (California: Ten Speed Press, 1981)

WEAVING A SAFETY NET

Many people never change their lives for the better, and it's not because they lack brains or motivation. Instead, they lack *support*. Pressure from others to "stay the way you are," the force of habit, and those inevitable moments of weak resolve can wear down even the most enthusiastic and determined individual.

Making changes solo is tough going. We *need* other people. We need them to encourage us, celebrate with us, cry with us, and give us a good swift kick in the pants when it's called for.

Relationships help us to deal with fear, frustration, stress, isolation, and other blocks to personal growth. Together they form a "safety net" which gives us the freedom to take risks and experiment with new behaviors.

When you're teetering along a tightrope, it's great to know that there's something beneath you to break your fall. Like people who love and accept you for the daredevil you are.

THE CURSE OF THE PIONEER SPIRIT

Unfortunately, our culture prefers that we go through life without a safety net. We get regular messages to be strong, be independent, go it alone, hide our feelings, and keep on trucking. It's all part of the "pioneer spirit" — the spirit that made us a great country full of lonely people.

Our culture also places a high value on winning — being first and beating others in pursuit of our goals. So we're a whole lot better at being aggressive than being supportive, at stuffing our pain and fear than sharing it.

We long for healthy relationships, but many of us (especially kids from troubled families) don't even know what healthy relationships are. As a result, we end up . . .

. . . having friends without really knowing them,

. . . putting on a good face, bending the truth, and never discussing the things that frighten or embarrass us,

. . . never hearing how wonderful, competent, and fascinating we are, and

. . . never knowing what it's like to have someone around who's truly interested in the details of our lives.

"[We] settle for superficial relationships. This occurs not only in the case of casual acquaintances, but even with members of our own families . . . . Consequently, we ourselves do not grow, nor do we help anyone else to grow. Meanwhile we have to live with repressed emotions — a dangerous and self-destructive path to follow."
John Powell in *Why Am I Afraid To Tell You Who I Am?*

The skills necessary to be a supportive person, function within a supportive relationship, and create a supportive NET-work for yourself don't come naturally. They must be learned, and they must be practiced.

BUILDING SUPPORTIVE RELATIONSHIPS

There are four specific skills you need to weave yourself a safety net:

1 The ability to express your feelings,

2 The ability to listen openly and noncritically,

3 The ability to offer positive feedback to others, and

4 The ability to ask for the support you need when you need it.

All have something important in common: *communication.*

> **"Any relationship, which is to have the nature of true personal encounter, must be based on this honest, open, gut-level communication. The alternative is to remain in my prison, to endure inch-by-inch death as a person."**
> John Powell in *Why Am I Afraid To Tell You Who I Am?*

Good communication requires a well-developed emotional vocabulary. Because talking about feelings is not a part of most people's daily lives, they lack the vocabulary needed to do it.

If you can't express your feelings, others can never really know you. They can know what you do and think, but not *who you are*. The inability to communicate feelings prohibits closeness.

Even worse, you can never know yourself. So not only are you cut off from other people; you're cut off from *you*.

"My greatest fear is to go through life without any real friends."
Holly (17)

THE FIVE LEVELS OF INTIMACY

Think for a moment about your relationships. Are there people you feel especially close to? People you know and like who know and like you back, people you call when you have problems or want to have some fun? If you had to grade your relationships, which would you give an "I" for intimacy?

Intimacy is another name for closeness, and it's a word that scares a lot of people. Actually, it encompasses several different types of friendships, not all of soul-mate intensity. An "intimacy scale" might look like this:

LOW INTIMACY	NORMAL INTIMACY	HIGH INTIMACY

1......................2...................... 3......................4...................... 5

If you put your relationships on this scale (with 1 being least intimate and 5 being most intimate), you'd probably find that most of your friends fall somewhere between 2 and 3. The 1s and 2s you might label "casual acquaintances;" the 4s and 5s are the truly special people in your life.

One way to assess the degree of intimacy in your relationships is by listening for the kinds of things you talk about and the ways in which you express yourself.

● **Level 1** relationships deal with FACTS — safe, nonthreatening, objective information about tests, the team, or the car that has little or nothing to do with the person behind the words. You spend a lot of classroom time on Level 1.

● **Level 2** relationships involve OTHER PEOPLE'S OPINIONS — also pretty safe. This is "they say" territory. "They say it's going to rain," "I hear Debby has a new boyfriend," and "The reviewer says the play is terrible" are all examples of Level 2-type talk.

They won't get you into trouble because you're not responsible for the content. (And they won't make it any easier for other people to get to know you.)

● **Level 3** relationships enter I THINK land. Here you offer subjective opinions about facts: "I don't like the color of her hair," "I think the music is awful," "I like your new car." The other person gets to know you from an intellectual perspective, which gives him or her a little piece of you to hold onto and remember. Level 3 begins to require some risk-taking because you open yourself up to conflict or rejection.

● **Level 4** relationships venture into FEELINGS. You use a feelings vocabulary and experience the feelings you're describing; a listener on the same level will also experience those feelings. For example, you might find yourself telling a friend how sad you are about the breakup of a relationship; you might share your anger or anxiety at getting a bad grade; you might cry together at a happy/sad movie. Joy and pain, fear and excitement become part of the communication. Since it's far more risky to share from your heart than your head, you become quite vulnerable — *and* you start feeling genuinely connected to the other person.

● **Level 5** relationships expose the SELF. They involve the most disclosure, the greatest risk, and the deepest sharing, and they require a high degree of confidence and trust in the other person. Being a 5 means revealing your feelings about the person you're with — love, fury, hurt, frustration, happiness, sadness, awe, sexual arousal, shyness, whatever. It's not easy to do, and it requires that you be in touch with your feelings, be able to express them (vocabulary!), and be willing to risk sharing yourself with your friend.

A Level 5 relationship isn't something you can demand or impose. It must evolve, and it takes time. If you spend long enough in a Level 4 relationship and put enough into it, there's a good chance it will move up into a Level 5. But first the relationship must prove trustworthy and both parties must make a commitment to it.

Let's add this new information to our intimacy scale:

LOW INTIMACY	NORMAL INTIMACY	HIGH INTIMACY		
1	2	3	4	5
FACTS	THEY SAY	I THINK	I FEEL	I AM

Would you change any of the ratings you made earlier? Are some of the relationships you thought were Level 5s really Level 4s or below? Is there a relationship you'd like to move from Level 3 to Level 4? What can you do to facilitate that?

Progressing from Level 1 to Level 5 means getting more and more involved with another person. As you might expect, there's a rule of sorts that governs people's behavior in very intimate relationships: If you want it to happen, and if you want it to last, you must give it proper care and feeding. You've probably heard that relationships take work; it's true!

The goal is not to turn *all* of your relationships into 5s, however. You wouldn't want to be best friends with everyone you know; that would be exhausting and overwhelming. A more appropriate goal is to develop the capacity to be a 4 or a 5 yourself, and then respond to each situation with the appropriate degree of intimacy.

Besides, we all need 1s and 2s in our lives. It's neither healthy nor desirable to be intense with everyone we meet. People we may never be truly close to can still provide us with diversity, knowledge, and a different kind of support. For example, if you're about to learn something new (like how to use a computer), it's useful to have a 1 around who's good with computers and willing to help.

But it's the 4s and 5s who hold up your safety net. And it's your ability to be a 4 or a 5 for them that makes them willing to do it.

GIVE-AND-GET

You've heard that relationships involve give-and-take; a better way to phrase this is "give-and-get." When you give of yourself, here's what you get in return:

- the opportunity to become more familiar with your feelings;

- the chance to develop a larger feelings vocabulary;

- connections with people who validate your self-worth and competency;

- the catharsis that comes from sharing your experiences and feelings (and relieving some of the pressure behind the dam);

- a noncritical ear, and the encouragement to talk and feel safe;

- honest feedback;

- nurturing (and a hug when you need it);

- acceptance for who you are; and

- the freedom and security that comes from trusting and being trusted.

"The deepest principle in human nature is the craving to be appreciated."
William James

If you want to know more about expressing feelings and building supportive relationships, read:

Why Am I Afraid To Tell You Who I Am? by John Powell (Illinois: Argus Communications, 1969)

The Angry Book by Theodore I. Rubin, M.D. (New York: Collier Books, 1970)

Wellness Workbook by Regina S. Ryan and John Travis (California: Ten Speed Press, 1981)

TAKING CHARGE OF YOUR LIFE

Have you ever felt as if life is like a ride on a tandem bicycle — and you're permanently stuck on the second seat? There you are, cruising down the highway, and all you get to do is pedal. Whenever you try to look straight ahead, someone else's back blocks your view.

Maybe you sometimes ask yourself, "Where am I going? Why am I going there? Who's in the driver's seat?" And maybe you bury these questions because they're too scary or hard to answer. Meanwhile, the stress inside you builds.

If you're not in charge of the travel plans, the only decision you'll get to make is how hard to pedal. If you're following someone else's itinerary, sooner or later the journey will lose its meaning and cease to be stimulating. What used to be an adventure will become boring, empty, a drag.

> "To drift is to be in hell; to be in heaven is to steer."
> George Bernard Shaw

Many of the decisions about your life will be made by other people, whether overtly or covertly. *They* will determine what school you attend, what classes you have to take, how late you can stay out, what chores around the house will be yours, and so on. Some of these decisions may be negotiable, but most will not.

You can probably go along with the majority without sacrificing too much. The ones you need to worry about are the Big Decisions about who you are and what you will do with your life.

It's great if there are people around to offer you options and provide guidance and support. But parents have been known to get carried away. They misinterpret their role and attempt to mold kids into what *they* want them to be.

Let's say the whole family is nuts for hockey. Dad played it, Oldest Son plays it, and Mom is at rinkside for every game. Chances are good that poor Junior will be "born with a puck in his mouth." The pressure (subtle and direct) will begin while he's still a babe. He may never get the chance to decide for himself if he even *likes* hockey.

Big Decisions are often a behind-the-scenes part of your world. Someone else quietly determines who you'll be and invites you to sit on the back of the bike. You want to do well, you want to please your parents, and you want people to like you, so you pedal like crazy. Every few miles you get rewarded for being good.

If the rewards are sufficient (lots of praise, a big allowance, the keys to the family car), you may never ask where you're going and why. Instead, you'll strive to live up to other people's expectations — and leave the control of your self-esteem in their hands.

How can you take charge of your own life? First, *you have to know when Big Decisions are being made for you.* And second, *you have to know how to write your own script.*

"There are really only two ways to approach life — as victim or as gallant fighter — and you must decide if you want to act or react, deal your own cards or play with a stacked deck. And if you don't decide which way to play with life, it always plays with you."
Merle Shain

"My greatest fear is that I will grow up unhappy and not do any of the things I want to do."
Sharon (16)

RECOGNIZING THE BIG DECISIONS

When someone makes a Big Decision for you, he or she often keeps you so busy with smaller decisions that you don't realize what's happening.

For example: For many bright kids, going to college is a Big Decision. But instead of being asked if they want to go, they're told, "You're going!" They may get to exercise some say in where to go, what to major in, and whether to live on or off campus. It's also possible that the only decision they'll get to make is how hard to study. ("Naturally, you'll go to Yale. We went there, and your grandparents went there. It's all settled.")

You can plug just about anything else into this example: being smart, being musical, being a jock, working in the family business. The content doesn't matter; it's the *process* that counts. And if you don't play a role in it from the beginning, you lose ground fast.

No matter how good something looks to someone else, it's worthless to *you* if *you* don't like it. There's nothing quite as tragic as a life devoid of meaning and challenge. (Although there *is* some comfort in just pedaling. At least you can blame someone else if the journey goes wrong!)

The following exercise can help you find out about the Big Decisions in your life. Plan to do it at a time when you can sit down and think without being interrupted.

a. List the important goals and directions for your life. (Straight As? A starring role in the school play? College? A career as a doctor? A family of your own?)

b. For each item on your list, ask yourself whether it was a *conscious* choice on your part — or whether "it's always been that way."

c. Make a separate list of the "always-been-that-ways."

d. For each item on this list, try to figure out when the decision was made and who made it.

You may discover that one person has consistently played the part of Big Decider. For most kids, it's a parent.

Can you think of any Big Decisions that are coming up soon? Try talking to the Big Decider in advance. Go into the discussion prepared to discuss what *you* want and why. It may help to use this as an icebreaker:

FOR PARENTS ONLY

We support you in wanting the best for your children, and this book has been written with that in mind.

One of the hardest lessons parents can learn is that their experience isn't always relevant to their children's lives. The pace at which the world is changing practically guarantees that. This doesn't invalidate what you went through; it just means that it may not be a suitable blueprint for your kids.

One of the greatest gifts parents can offer their children is exposure to a broad range of experiences — and the encouragement to develop their own capacity for personal choice. The earlier young people start accepting responsibility for the consequences of their choices, the sooner they gain the confidence needed to deal with life in *their* jungle.

WRITING YOUR OWN SCRIPT

Imagine that your life is a movie — and you get to write the script. You may not be able to direct every scene, but at least you can decide what happens and when.

This takes courage. If you're going to make choices, then you're also going to have to take responsibility for them. If the movie turns out to be a dud, you'll take the fall. Then again, it may end up winning the Academy Award for Best Picture. The joy, satisfaction, and self-confidence that come from seeing your goals become realities can be very rewarding.

Writing your life's script involves four steps:

1. Creating a Personal Vision of what *you* want your life to be,

2. Planning for diversity,

3. Bringing the future into the present, and

4. Deciding what's important for *today*.

Creating a Personal Vision

For many kids, the plan for their life involves nothing more than getting good grades. But while getting straight As is certainly a commendable goal, it's only *one* goal. By putting all of your self-esteem eggs into the academic basket, you run the risk of suffering a major life crisis should you ever fail to meet your expectations.

Besides, there will come a day when you're no longer in school (hard to believe, but true!). Then what? If getting good grades is all you know how to do, you won't be prepared for much of anything else.

Your Personal Vision should extend beyond today, beyond tomorrow, into years too far ahead to see. You should start thinking now about the kind of person you want to be in your 20s, your 30s, your 40s . . . maybe even your 70s and 80s. Why not? It's YOUR life!

Get in the mood by trying this exercise: On a piece of paper, list all of the things you want to have accomplished by age 70.
In creating your Personal Vision, don't let ANYTHING (real or imagined) hold you back. And don't be afraid to dream!

Here are some broad questions to start off with:

◆ Will I continue my education after high school? How and where?

◆ Will I travel someday? Where and when?

◆ Will I marry and have children?

◆ What kind of relationship will I have with my parents?

◆ How will I earn my living?

◆ What kinds of friends will I have? What kinds will I want?

◆ What hobbies will I develop?

◆ What will I be known for?

◆ How will I develop my spirituality?

◆ How will I be different from the way I am today?

◆ What will I do to keep myself healthy?

◆ What will be important to me?

Write your responses in a notebook or your journal, if you're in the habit of keeping one (maybe this is a good time to start). Don't worry if you can't answer all of the questions right now, or if the answers you come up with aren't the greatest. Both the questions and your responses will change as you learn more about life and yourself.

Repeat this exercise at regular intervals, refining your vision as needed to make room for the new, growing you.

Planning for Diversity

Diversity keeps you interested and interesting. Your Personal Vision should include things you've never tried — maybe never even considered trying because you can't be sure of a positive return.

A lot of kids have trouble with this. They can't see beyond the things they know they can do. They dig ruts for themselves — and a rut is just a long, skinny grave. The harder they work, the deeper they get and the less of the world they see.

There's nothing wrong with doing the things you do best. Proving your competence over and over leads to self-esteem. If that's *all* you do, however, you'll never develop the strong self-esteem (and courage) that comes from being capable in many different areas.

When we asked some kids to describe some things they wanted to try — and what they thought was holding them back — here is what they said:

"I'd like to pack up sometime, grab a friend or two, and hit the road for a couple of days." *What's stopping you?* "My parents wouldn't like it, and I don't have a car." (Lynn, 16)

"I wish I could try a new personality." *What's stopping you?* "A lot of people like the one I have." (Heather, 12)

"I think about writing a story and sending it to a publisher." *What's stopping you?* "Fear of rejection." (Kelly, 15)

"I'd like to try scuba diving." *What's stopping you?* "My mom would probably have a heart attack." (Holly, 17)

"Anything." *What's stopping you?* "Me." (Kathy, 13)

"I'm interested in hang gliding." *What's stopping you?* "I'm not old enough for lessons, and I'm scared of heights." (Laura, 14)

> "When so little of the physical and mental as well as the innate spiritual vitality of person and culture is being tapped, when too great a reliance is being placed on the rational, the immediate, and the functional, then consciousness is caught in tunnel vision, inadequate to deal with the complexities and challenges of the time. Thus we recognize the tragic consequences of this inadequacy and our present seeming inability to use the range of what we are."
> Jean Houston, in *The Possible Human*

Bringing the Future Into the Present

Your Personal Vision contains numerous goals, both stated and implied. If you wrote, "I will earn my living as an astronaut," that includes your ultimate goal (completing the astronaut training program) as well as many other goals leading up to it (learning the requirements for the program, going to college, keeping physically fit, developing a specialty, applying to the program, etc.)

In other words, you won't get into astronaut training simply by wishing yourself there. You'll need to develop — and follow — a plan.

It's not to soon to start planning for each of your Personal Vision goals. (Remember that if you don't get involved in the process, someone else may make your decisions for you. And you may find yourself pedaling straight into law school!)

Your plan should include the following:

■ a goal statement;

■ a list of the steps leading up to your goal;

■ a list of roadblocks and ways of getting around them;

■ a list of resources that can help you to achieve your goal; and

■ criteria you can use to measure your progress along the way.

Let's use an example to illustrate how this works. Assume that one of your Personal Vision goals is to stay physically fit throughout your life. Here's how your plan might turn out:

1 GOAL STATEMENT

To start a physical activity program.

2 GOAL DEVELOPMENT STEPS

▲ Make a list of why "getting physical" will be good for me and post it on the wall in my room

▲ Make a list of the physical activities I might enjoy

▲ Talk to people who are familiar with these activities

▲ Find out what equipment I'd need for each and how much it would cost

▲ Choose one activity

▲ Design an easy program to get started on

▲ Find other people who have the same interest

3 ROADBLOCKS

WHAT MIGHT HAPPEN:	WHAT I CAN DO:
My friends will make fun of me.	*Get support from new people; check out some books on the subject; find a training partner; learn to deal with people who make fun of me.*
The equipment I need will turn out to be too expensive.	*Find ways to make extra money; figure out what to do until I can afford good equipment; borrow equipment; get a loan from my parents.*
I'll start doing it, but my lazy nature and lack of self-discipline will ultimately win out.	*Develop a weekly schedule and post it in my room; don't over-challenge myself; plan on some rewards for mileposts; be sure to have a training partner.*

4 RESOURCES

◆ Library books on the subject

◆ Ask Jill about her jogging group

◆ Find out where Tom gets his athletic shoes

◆ Get information on the President's Council on Physical Fitness

◆ Talk to phy-ed teacher

5 CRITERIA

I'll know my program is working when:

- I do my activity three times a week no matter what
- I feel better about myself
- I start losing some excess weight
- I have more energy
- My training partner and I have established a normal routine

It takes time to go through this process with each of your life goals. But unless you make specific plans, your Personal Vision will never be more than wishful thinking. Like the carrot in front of the donkey, it will keep leading you on without getting any closer.

Deciding What's Important for Today

The more you reach out for new experiences, the more opportunities and options you will have. This happy thought can be a nightmare in disguise if you already feel overwhelmed by all of the things you have to do.

Many of the kids we talked to reported that there was "too much going on" in their lives and they didn't know how they'd get it all done. They believed that they *had* to stay on top of everything or face horrible consequences. Several reported increased amounts of stress and worry due to procrastination. In short, they had become their own worst tigers!

If you've been growing whiskers and a tail, there's an alternative to turning yourself in at the local zoo. It's called *time management*. It can help you to sort through your goals and options, decide

what's important for TODAY, and tackle each one in turn.

Time management organizes the various pieces of your life into a series of small, manageable steps. It also ensures that you keep your long-term goals in mind. (That's how your Personal Vision becomes a reality.)

"Without discipline, there's no life at all."
Katharine Hepburn

The key to time management is prioritizing your activities. There are many different ways to approach this. One that we especially like is called the "ABC" method. Here's how it works:

1. Make a "things-to-do" list. Go back to your Personal Vision goals and choose two or three activities from each that you could do today.

Here's an example:
Do something fun with the guys
Write a letter to Aunt Erma
Get information on the college entrance exam
Write paper for Friday's history class
Shop for running shoes
Get sister's birthday present
Listen to relaxation tape
Go to library to start researching English paper due next week
Go for 2-mile walk with Ann
Call for job interview

2. Now rank each item on your list according to this scale:
   A (for Very Important, Must Be Done)
   B (for Kind Of Important, Can Wait)
   C (for Nice But Not Essential)

Let's say that one of your most important goals is to decrease the amount of stress in your life. As a result, regular relaxation is a high-priority item for you. You want to *make* time for it, not *find* time for it after everything else is done. So "Listen to relaxation tapes" and "Do something fun with the guys" will both be As.

You also have two papers due soon: a history one for this Friday, and an English one for next week. Obviously the history paper will take precedence. You'll give it an A, and your up-front work for your English paper will get a B.

Your list looks like this:

A Do something fun with the guys
C Write a letter to Aunt Erma
B Get information on the college entrance exam
A Write paper for Friday's history class
C Shop for running shoes
B Get sister's birthday present
A Listen to relaxation tape
B Go to library to start researching English paper due next week
B Go for 2-mile walk with Ann
A Call for job interview

3● **Next, rank all of your As, Bs, and Cs individually** (since you have several of each). The most important A should be assigned an A-1 ranking; the next most important, A-2; and so on.

Here's what you come up with:

A-4 Do something fun with the guys
C-2 Write a letter to Aunt Erma
B-4 Get information on the college entrance exam
A-1 Write paper for Friday's history class
C-1 Shop for running shoes
B-2 Get sister's birthday present
A-3 Listen to relaxation tape
B-3 Go to library to start researching English paper due next week
B-1 Go for 2-mile walk with Ann
A-2 Call for job interview

At this point, you *know* which items are top priority and which can wait. You can start attacking them methodically and systematically. When you've finished the As, start on the Bs.

Two tips to keep in mind along the way:

▼ The goal is NOT to accomplish everything on your list. If that's how things work out, terrific, but don't push it. Just do the best you can in the time you have available.

▼ Don't treat your list as if it's cast in concrete. Your priorities will change from one day to the next, and sometimes from one minute to the next. (For example, you learn that the due date on your history paper has been pushed back a week. Or your friend Ann has a scheduling conflict and can't go for a walk until tomorrow.)

Putting your plans into action absolutely *requires* that you manage your time. And managing your time means knowing what you have to do and when you have to do it.

Making a list gives you a sense of direction. But that's not sufficient. Unless you rank the items on it, you're left with an assortment of "got tos," all of which seem to have the same value — which leads to the "do-everything-today-or-else" mentality and long-term stress.

Planning and prioritizing will put you in charge of your life and create a feeling of accomplishment all by itself. Each step you take will bring you closer of your vision of who you want to be.

> "Time is life. It is irreversible and irreplaceable. To waste your time is to waste your life, but to master your time is to master your life and make the most of it."
> Alan Lakein in *How To Get Control of Your Time and Your Life*

A SHORT COURSE ON RISK-TAKING

Which would you rather do . . . .

. . . spend the weekend studying for an upcoming exam, or go to a party where you won't know anyone?

. . . take on a project for extra credit, or plan a canoe trip with new friends?

In each case, the second option poses a risk. Taking a risk is like going on a dangerous journey. You don't know what you'll encounter along the way, and you won't be able to draw on your knowledge or experience to see you through.

Plus there are two nasty critters that can interrupt your journey: the Wouldbut and the Whatif. Either one can jump out and bite you at any moment. And when it does, you'll find yourself saying things like, "Well, I *would* do that, *but* . . . " or "I *could* do that, but *what if* . . . . "

How can you fight off the Wouldbut and Whatif? By knowing how to take risks in a way that practically guarantees success. And that requires learning some risk-taking skills.

1 **Start small.**

Don't focus on the end of your journey, but on how you're going to get there: one step at a time.

For example: You've decided that you want to be a skier. (Maybe your Personal Vision includes skiing the Alps someday.) What's the first thing you should do — head for the nearest mountain and hop aboard the ski lift? That wouldn't do much for your self-confidence.

Instead, get a book on skiing from your local library. Join the school ski club, if there is one, or arrange to take a beginner's course at a nearby resort. You'll learn about the sport and make new friends besides.

Reading a book is no risk at all. Joining the ski club or taking a course involves some risk, but it's one that everyone else will share. Familiarity with the sport and the reassurance of your new friends will give you the confidence you need to hit the slopes for the first time. From then on, all that will stand between you and the Alps will be plenty of practice!

2 Give yourself permission to be average or worse.

This is tough for kids who are used to excelling. But if you're starting something that's totally new to you, you probably *won't* be good at it right away. For a change, plan to underachieve! (You may want to write notes to yourself to read when you're feeling like an incompetent toad.)

3 Get support.

Find four or five people who will give you help and encouragement. Meet with them regularly and invite their comments and constructive feedback.

There will be times when your enthusiasm weakens or you get disgusted and feel like quitting. Everyone has moments like these. Understanding friends can give you the strength to weather them and go on to the next stage of your risk-taking.

4 Celebrate yourself.

Rejoice at *any* success, no matter how small or insignificant it may seem. Remember that big changes don't happen all at once. Instead, they're the result of consistently meeting lesser and more manageable goals.

Design a reward system for yourself. Throw a party, or simply pat yourself on the back. You deserve it!

"You must do the thing you think you cannot do."
Eleanor Roosevelt

THE BURDEN OF PERFECTIONISM

The trouble with being a perfectionist is that your self-worth is continually on the line. You can't enjoy an activity unless you're outstanding at it. If you fail at something, your ego comes crashing down. So you hesitate to take risks because you can't foresee the results.

Perfectionism is a major roadblock to progress. It keeps you locked into the things you know you can do. Taken to an extreme, it can prevent you from ever trying *anything* new. And that severely limits the scope of your Personal Vision (while making you boring besides).

Are *you* a perfectionist? The following exercise can help you to find out more about that side of yourself.

Decide how much you agree with each statement. Then fill in the blank beside it with one of these numbers:

> +2 (for "I agree very much")
> +1 (for "I agree somewhat")
> 0 (for "I feel neutral about this")
> −1 (for "I disagree slightly")
> −2 (for "I disagree strongly")

___ If I don't set the highest standards for myself, I am likely to end up a second-rate person.

___ People will think less of me if I make mistakes.

— If I can't do something really well, there's little point in doing it at all.
— I should be upset if I make a mistake.
— If I try hard enough, I should be able to excel at anything I attempt to do.
— It is shameful for me to display any weakness or childish behaviors.
— I shouldn't have to repeat the same mistake more than once.
— An average performance is bound to be unsatisfying to me.
— Failing at something important makes me less of a person.
— If I scold myself for failing to live up to my expectations, it will help me to do better the next time.

Now total your score. Plus and minus numbers cancel each other out.

An above-zero score indicates a tendency toward perfectionism. A below-zero score signifies a less perfectionist mindset.

If you think you may be a perfectionist, you need to find ways to develop some objectivity about yourself. Use these for starters:

■ Decide how much time you're going to spend on a given project, and stick to it. (For the perfectionist, no amount of effort is ever enough.) Practice saying, "It's time to stop; I've done a good job; now I'll go on to something else."

■ Reward yourself for being *in the process* of learning a new activity, regardless of your performance.

■ Redefine the word "mistake" in your own mind. Instead of letting it stand for failure, try thinking of it as proof that you're learning and growing.

If you want to know more about overcoming perfectionism, read:
Feeling Good by David Burns, M.D. (New York: Signet Books, 1981).
Dr. Burns offers tremendous insight into the problems of perfectionism. The exercise used above was adapted from his work.

GROWING A FUNNY BONE

After all of the serious stuff you've been reading, you're probably in the mood for a laugh. Great, because that's directly related to yet another form of stress management.

As you develop your lifeskills, more will go right in your life and you'll experience less stress. You'll feel lighter, happier, and more like laughing.

There's a physiological reason for this: As stress starts to fade, your funny bone starts to grow.

You probably didn't know that. You may not even believe that you *have* a funny bone. And you thought you knew human anatomy!

What's the precise location of this wonderful appendage? Actually, different people have them in different places. It all depends on where they're most ticklish. The bottom of the foot seems to be the most common place, although funny bones have also been found between ribs and even under arms.

It doesn't really matter where yours is. What matters is that you have one. A funny bone can help to keep things in perspective when life is being particularly confusing or nasty. A sense of humor, frequent laughter, and some solid playtime are essential to a healthy sense of who you are and what life is all about.

Ever since a man named Norman Cousins cured himself of a terminal disease by watching funny films, scientists have been studying the therapeutic benefits of having a sense of humor. According to Dr. William Fry of Stanford University, laughter increases one's respiratory activity, oxygen exchange, muscular activity, and heart rate. It stimulates the cardiovascular system, the sympathetic nervous system, and the pituitary gland and leads to a positive biochemical state.

It appears that the more you laugh, the better you feel. And the better you feel, the more you laugh. At last: a *positive* vicious circle!

"If it's not fun, don't do it!"
Don Ardell in *Planning for Wellness: A Guidebook for Achieving Optimal Health*

Here are some tips for growing an enormous funny bone:

- Surround yourself with people who have a good sense of humor — people who can make you laugh and feel happy with them.

- Go to funny movies. Don't neglect the oldies but goodies: Charlie Chaplin, the Three Stooges, Laurel & Hardy, the fabulous Marx Brothers.

- Watch funny TV. (This really is a matter of taste. To some people, the soaps are hilarious.)

- Read funny books. There are scores of writers capable of making you laugh out loud. What about Mark Twain, or Bruce Jay Friedman? Dorothy Parker? Ogden Nash? Robert Benchley? William Thurber?

- Listen to comedy albums.

- If at all possible, go to live comedy shows. There's never been a better time for stand-up comedy.

- Practice your smile in front of a mirror. Laugh out loud into a recorder, and play it back when you feel blue.

- Learn a joke a week and share it with everyone you know.

- Laugh whenever and wherever you get the chance.

Some 70 years ago, a man named Bernarr Macfadden (one of the first psychophysiologists) waxed poetic about laughter and its healing properties. His words, from his book *Vitality Supreme*, are worth repeating here:

Many a man, placed in a trying situation, would have been saved from tragical consequences if he could have found some means of arousing the emotions expressed in a good hearty laugh. The inclination to stimulate the emotions associated with laughter and good humor should be encouraged at every opportunity.

There is no question that laughter has valuable vitalizing qualities. It undoubtedly adds to one's stamina. It gives one a hopeful spirit. It leads one to look upon the bright side of life. When you can laugh, the sun is shining regardless of how many clouds obscure the sky.

Mr. Macfadden then went on to offer the following instructions on how to laugh:

A. *The bodily expression and mechanical efforts that go with happiness will often induce the feelings and emotions associated therewith. To prove the accuracy of this statement, some morning when you are feeling especially gloomy and unpleasant, look into your mirror and go through the process of trying to make yourself smile. Screw up your features in such a manner as to force the required contractions of the facial muscles. If you continue your efforts long enough you will surely be rewarded by a real smile and with all the sense of good cheer that a smile will bring.*

B. *First of all assume a laughing position, in order to laugh properly and to secure the best results. Stand with the feet far apart, and with the knees slightly bent. Now bring the palms of the hands down and 'slap' them vigorously on the legs just above the knees, and then swing your bent arms overhead, making a noise as nearly as possible like laughing. Yes, you are quite right, it will sound very much like a cold stage laugh at first, and you will have to force it, but as you go on with the experiment it will gradually* become more natural. Continue this long enough and I defy anyone to differentiate the emotions aroused from those associated with a real, spontaneous laugh.

He suggests that if you can practice among companions, you will soon have them "guffawing loudly and violently."

Although this gentleman was ahead of his time, his advice seems especially suited to ours. Research carried out by the Laughter Project at the University of California in Santa Barbara revealed that laughter did as well at reducing stress as complex biofeedback training programs. And, as the researchers pointed out, laughter requires no special training, no special equipment, and no special laboratory conditions. It's easy, it's free, and all it takes is a funny bone.

"Strange, when you come to think of it, that of all the countless folk who have lived before our time on this planet not one is known in history or in legend as having died of laughter."
Max Beerbohm

AFTERWORD: NOW WHAT?

We hope that this look at "the jungle" has made it more understandable and less frightening and stressful for you.

We also hope that you have a revitalized and expanded sense of your own potential. Put your new knowledge and lifeskills to work for you, and there's no telling how far you can go.

Imagine a lifetime of . . . .

. . . improving physical health,
. . . growing support systems and an increasing capacity for intimacy in your relationships,
. . . near immunity to manipulation by others,
. . . more control over your own experiences,
. . . a heightened ability to communicate your needs and feelings,
. . . a strong sense of personal direction,
. . . diversity and variety in your activities,
. . . the ability to organize and prioritize your life,
. . . the freedom to shape your life in such a way as to make it meaningful and relevant to you, AND
. . . unlimited success.

We have purposely made this scenario idealistic. Why not; you're used to shooting for the stars!

Now for a few words of caution: *You* may change, but the world won't always be on your side. Lifeskills training is not yet a part of our culture. Ironically, it's only *after* kids have reached their limits of coping ability and chosen destructive behaviors to deal with stress that they're offered skill-building and support group activities — for "rehabilitation!" More band-aids on tiger bites.

We are conditioned to accept "the system" and adapt to it. Our culture invites us to accept a life of high stress and low satisfaction. What we're saying is that you may not get much support for your decision to make things better for yourself. In fact, you may meet with a great deal of resistance.

In reading this book, you've taken a valuable first step. You now have a sense of what life *could* be for you — and some skills needed to effect real changes. It's a start! Ideally, you'll find ways to continue learning, to keep growing, to never stop trying to be your best.

Some last-minute tips to speed you on your way out of the jungle:

- Have the courage to dream big dreams for your life.
- Be serious about *your* needs and agenda.
- Take the risks necessary to make your dreams come true.
- Trust your intuition — about people, about the right directions to take and decisions to make.
- Find people who will help and support you. Look for good role models.
- Use your creativity and intelligence to make "the system" work for you.
- Write to me c/o Free Spirit Publishing and let me know how you're doing. Tell me about your problems and your successes. I'm still learning, too.

You *can* make things happen, you *can* open new doors, you *can* make a difference, you *can* be responsible, you *can* start THIS MINUTE!

"I want you to get excited about who you are, what you are, what you have, and what can still be for you. I want to inspire you to see that you can go far beyond where you are right now."
Virginia Satir in *Peoplemaking*

INDEX